monday morning

Super-Duper Science

Amazing Animals!

by Annalisa McMorrow

illustrated by Marilynn G. Barr

For Catherine & Tiger

Publisher: Roberta Suid
Copy Editor: Carol Whiteley
Design & Production: Scott McMorrow
Cover Art: Mike Artell
Cover Design: David Hale
Educational Consultant: Tanya Lieberman

Also by the author: *Save the Animals!* (MM1964), *Love the Earth!* (MM1965), *Learn to Recycle!* (MM1966), *Sing a Song About Animals* (MM1987), *Preschool Connections* (MM1993), *Incredible Insects! (And Spiders, Too)* (MM2018), *Spectacular Space!* (MM2019), *Outstanding Oceans!* (MM2020), *Ladybug, Ladybug* (MM2015), *Twinkle, Twinkle* (MM2016), *Rub-a-Dub-Dub* (MM2017), *Daffy-Down-Dilly* (MM2037), *Pussycat, Pussycat* (MM2036), *Rain, Rain, Go Away!* (MM2038), *Peculiar Plants!* (MM2058), and *Wacky Weather!* (MM2057).

Entire contents copyright ©1998 by Monday Morning Books, Inc.
For a complete catalog, please write to the address below:

P.O. Box 1680
Palo Alto, CA 94302 U.S.A.

Call us at: 1-800-255-6049

E-mail us at: MMBooks@aol.com

Visit our Web site:
http://www.mondaymorningbooks.com

Monday Morning Books is a registered trademark of
Monday Morning Books, Inc.

ISBN 1-57612-045-7

Printed in the United States of America

987654321

Contents

Introduction: Why Animals?

Animals are talented (bats can tell how fast insects are traveling using sonar-like echolocation), famous (Koko the gorilla learned to communicate with sign language), tricky (a polar bear covers its black nose when stalking prey in order to blend with the snow), and all-around amazing!

Children will learn about the exciting animal world while practicing writing, reading, research, performance, and speaking skills. They'll learn how animals communicate, give pouch reports (featuring marsupials), measure a tiger, learn about colorblind lions, star in a musical review, and much more. Most of the activities can easily be simplified for younger children or extended for upper grades. This book will enhance learning in many subjects through exploration of the animals that share planet Earth with us.

Amazing Animals! is divided into four parts (plus a resource section). **Hands-On Discoveries** contains activities that allow children to participate in answering science questions they may have, for example, "How do zebras blend in?" or "How are bats' wings different from birds' wings?" Reproducible sheets have directions written specifically for the children. These sheets are marked with a special paw print icon.

Nonfiction Book Links features speaking, writing, and reporting activities based on nonfiction resources. Most activities are accompanied by helpful handouts that lead children through the research procedure. When research is required, you have the option of letting children look for the facts needed in the library (or in books you've checked out ahead of time). Or they may use the "Super-Duper Fact Cards" located in the resource section at the back of this book. These cards list information for unusual animals. Duplicate the cards onto neon-colored paper, and cut them out. Laminate the cards, and cut them out again, making sure to leave a thin laminate border to prevent peeling. Keep the cards in a box for children to choose from when doing their research. These cards also provide an opportunity for younger children to do research by giving them needed information in a simple, easy-to-understand format.

The **Fiction Book Links** section uses storybooks to introduce information about interesting animals. This section's activities, projects, and language extensions help children connect with fictional animals. Each "Link" also includes a tongue twister. You can challenge children to create their own twisters from the animal facts they've learned. Also included in this section are decorating suggestions for "setting the stage" for each particular book.

It's Show Time! presents chants, new songs sung to old tunes, and costume suggestions for putting on a performance. The songs can be duplicated and given to the children. If you want to hold a performance, write each performer's name on the reproducible program page and give copies to your audience.

Each of the first three sections ends with a "Super-Duper Project," an activity that uses the information children have learned in the unit. These projects include creating an animal mural, publishing an animal-fact newspaper, and writing new animal fables. A choral performance is a possible "Super-Duper" ending for the "It's Show Time!" section.

The last two pages of the book are nonfiction resources to share with children, and animal-related Web sites to explore.

Suggestions for Extending Lessons:

• If you divide your class into teams, have each team choose the name of an animal group, for example, the "Pride of Lions" group or the "Gang of Elks" group.
• Use patterns, such as elephants (p. 46) or marsupials (pp. 35-36), as name tags or desk labels.
• Take children on a field trip to a local zoo or wildlife park.
• Invite a representative from an animal shelter to speak to your children.
• Have children observe and report on animal life around them: cats, dogs, birds, and so on.

Amazing Animals! © 1998 Monday Morning Books, Inc.

All About Mammals

What Makes an Animal a Mammal?

All of the animals featured in this book are mammals. Mammals are warm-blooded animals. This means that their body temperatures stay just about the same, no matter how cold or warm their surroundings are. Because they have warm blood, mammals are warm to the touch.

Human beings are mammals. So are bats and cats and whales and kangaroos. Mother mammals produce milk for their babies to drink. Mammals have skeletons inside their bodies. A skeleton is a frame of bones held together by the backbone. Most mammals give birth to live babies, not to eggs. However, there are a few exceptions (see p. 37).

There are thousands of different kinds of mammals. All breathe air, even though some live in the water (whales, dolphins, manatees, and porpoises). Most mammals live on the land. Some mammals are carnivores. This means they eat other animals. Others are herbivores, which means they eat only plants. Insectivores eat mainly insects. Some mammals eat plants *and* animals. They're called omnivores.

The largest and heaviest mammal is the blue whale. The smallest mammal, not counting bats, is called Savi's white-toothed pygmy shrew. These animals are able to travel through tunnels left by large earthworms. The smallest bat is called the bumblebee bat and lives in Thailand.

Scale of Animal Sizes

Build-a-Bat

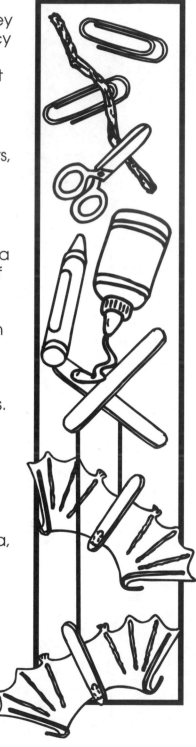

How do bats fly in the dark without bumping into anything? They use echolocation. This means that they send out high-frequency signals that hit an object and bounce back to the bats as echoes. The bats can tell how far away the object is, how big it is, and its texture. Dolphins and shrews also use echolocation.

Materials:
"Wing Patterns" (p. 9), black tissue paper, pipe cleaners, scissors, tape or glue, Popsicle sticks, crayons or markers

Directions:
1. Duplicate a copy of the "Wing Patterns" for each child.
2. Have children list the differences between a bat's wing and a bird's wing. Birds' wings are feathered. Bats' wings are made of thin skin. Bats have a short thumb with a strong claw at the tip. Birds don't have thumbs.
3. Give each child a Popsicle stick for a bat body. Children can decorate the sticks with crayons or markers.
4. Have children trace the bat wings onto tissue paper and cut out.
5. Using pipe cleaners, children can create fingers for the wings.
6. Have children glue or tape the tissue paper wings to the Popsicle stick bats.
7. Post the bats upside down on a bulletin board.

Options:
• Children can use a globe to find the places where bats live. (Bats live in many places around the world, including Africa, Australia, Malaysia, and North and South America.)
• Divide the children into pairs. Each team will make two bats, one representing the largest bat wingspan (5 ft./2 m.), and the other representing the smallest (6 in./16 cm.). Hang the finished bats upside down from a length of clothesline strung across the room.

Fun Fact:
In some cultures, bats are thought to be good luck. In China, bat images were used in the design of the emperor's throne.

Wing Patterns

Colorblind Lions

Zebras are herbivores, which means they eat plants. Lions are carnivores, which means they eat meat, such as zebras. However, lions (like many other animals) are colorblind. They see in black, white, and shades of grey. This helps the zebra to blend with its surroundings.

Materials:
"Colorblind Lions" Hands-on Handout (p. 11), "Animal Camouflage" Hands-on Handout (p. 12), "Zebra Patterns" (p. 13), crayons or markers (including black, green, and yellow), white construction paper, scissors, glue

Directions:
1. Duplicate one copy of the "Colorblind Lions" Hands-on Handout, the "Animal Camouflage" Hands-on Handout, and the "Zebra Patterns" for each child.
2. Discuss animal camouflaging with the students. Go over the different examples on the "Animal Camouflage" Hands-on Handout.
3. Have the children perform this camouflage experiment either singly or in small groups. (Directions for the activity are on the following page.)
4. Record the children's findings and have them share their discoveries with the rest of the class.
5. Post the finished pictures on a "Colorblind Lions" bulletin board.

Options:
• Children can make other pictures representing the animal camouflage techniques listed on the "Animal Camouflage" Hands-on Handout.
• Hold a costume party in which children dress as animals who use camouflage. Costumes can be made from paper grocery bags and tempera paint.

Fun Fact:
Male lions have manes. Lionesses don't.

Colorblind Lions

What You Need:
Crayons (black, green, yellow), white paper, "Zebra Patterns," scissors, glue

What You Do:
1. Use black crayons to draw a grassy field on white paper.
2. Use green and yellow crayons to draw another grassy field on another piece of paper.
3. Cut out the "Zebra Patterns" and glue one to each sheet of paper.
4. Answer the questions below.

Questions:
1. Which background does the zebra blend in with the best from your point of view?

_____

_____

2. Lions can only see in black and white. If lions could see in color, what colors might the zebra want to be?

_____

_____

Amazing Animals! © 1998 Monday Morning Books, Inc.

Animal Camouflage

• White polar bears blend in with their snowy surroundings. When a polar bear hunts, it covers its black nose with one paw so that it appears entirely white.

• Giraffes look brightly colored to us, with their yellow, brown, and tan bodies. But against a background of similarly colored leafy trees, giraffes blend right in!

• Okapis, relatives of the giraffe, have purple coats with white bands on their legs. They are very difficult to spot in the rain forest habitat.

• Black panthers blend in with shadows in the jungle.

• Many animals living in cold regions change their coats in the winter to blend in with snow. These include: ermines, snowshoe hares, and foxes.

• Green algae grows on a sloth's fur, helping the sloth blend in with the leaves in the trees it hangs from.

• Lions have golden fur that is a similar color to the grasses in the plains where they live.

Zebra Patterns

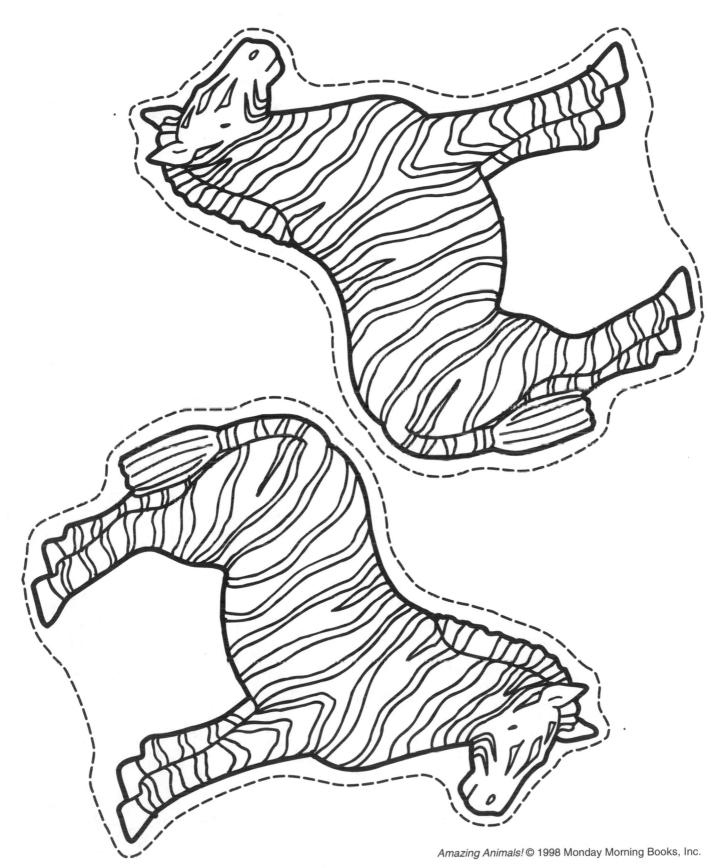

The Biggest Cat

The cat family includes leopards, lions, jaguars, cougars, pumas, house cats, and more. Big cats include only lions, tigers, leopards, and jaguars. Although lions are known as "the kings of the jungle," tigers are actually the biggest members of the cat family. They can weigh from 280 to 660 lbs. (130 to 300 kg.).

Materials:
"Tiger Pattern" (p. 15), overhead projector, butcher paper, tape measure, marker, scissors, black and orange tempera paint, paintbrushes

Directions:
1. Make a transparency from the "Tiger Pattern." Use it to project a large outline on a sheet of butcher paper. Measure the outline before tracing it—it should be at least 10 ft. (3 m.) long.
2. Trace the outline of the tiger and cut it out.
3. Have children use tempera paint and brushes to paint the tiger. Tigers are orange with black stripes.
4. Once the tiger dries, have the children measure the tiger and write the measurement on a piece of paper.
5. Post the tiger on a wall with the measurement listed below. You can add the following facts, as well: Adult male tigers average 10 ft. 3 in. (3.12 m.) and stand 39-42 in. (99-107 cm.) at the shoulder. The largest tiger supposedly measured 10 ft. 7 in. (3.22 m.).

Fun Fact:
Small cats purr but can't roar, and big cats roar but can't purr. (The exception is the snow leopard. If you hear it purr...watch out!)

Tiger Pattern

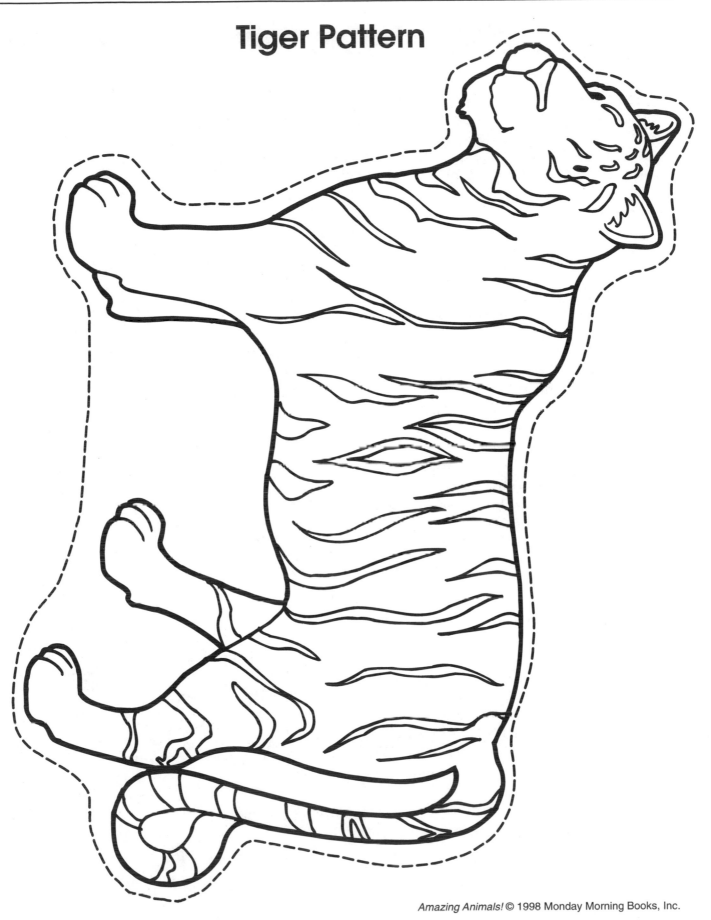

Hippo Family Album

Hippos are even-toed ungulates. An ungulate is a hoofed mammal. Each of the hippo's feet has four toes and each toe ends in a hoof-like nail. Although hippos are sometimes called "river horses," they're not related to horses. The hippo is related to the pig, peccary (wild pig), and crested boar.

Materials:

"Hippo Family Photos" (p. 17), crayons or markers, scissors, file folders (one per child), glue or glue stick, glitter pens

Directions:

1. Duplicate a copy of the "Hippo Family Photos" for each child.
2. Explain that all of the animals in these pictures are related.
3. Have each child make a Hippo Family Photo Album by coloring the patterns (brown or gray for the hippos, pink for the piglets, and shades of brown for the rest), cutting them out, and gluing them inside a file folder.
4. Children can decorate the outside of their folders with glitter pens or other decorations. They can draw their own pictures of hippos, or trace them from library books.
5. Invite children in other classes to look through the Hippo Family Photo Albums and guess the relationship of the animals. (Some children might not believe hippos are related to pigs!)

Options:

• Have children add facts beneath the photos that are taken from the "Super-Duper Fact Card" (p. 72) or other resource books.
• Children can make other "family" photo albums for the members of the cat family (see p. 14), the dog family (wolves, foxes, jackals, dingoes, coyotes, and so on), or the marsupials (see p. 34).
• For more on animal feet, check out *What Neat Feet!* by Shana Machotka (Morrow, 1991).

Fun Fact:

When hippos open their mouths wide, they're not yawning. They are showing that they're ready to fight!

Hippo Family Photos

Boar

Babirusa

Wart Hog

Piglet

Peccary

Hippopotamus

It's All Relative

Materials:
"Animal Playing Cards" (pp. 19-21), heavy paper, crayons or markers, scissors

Directions:
1. Duplicate the "Animal Playing Cards" onto heavy paper, color, and cut apart.
2. Laminate the playing cards and cut out again, leaving a thin laminate border to prevent peeling.
3. Teach children how to play the game. The object is to match families of animals. Children play the game like "Go Fish," looking for sets of three. Instead of the pictures matching exactly, the animals only have to be relatives. For example, a hippo and a pig and a peccary would make a set, as would a donkey, a zebra, and a horse.

How to Play the Game:
• Shuffle the cards and deal four to each player.
• Place the rest of the cards face down in a stack.
• If children have any sets (three animals in the same family) in their hands at the start, they lay the sets face up in front of them.
• One child begins. This player asks any of the other children for any of the animals in one of the families in his or her hand. For example, this first player might ask, "Do you have any animals in the pig family?" If the other player has pig family cards, all must be given to the first player.
• If the first player receives a card (or cards), he or she can ask anyone for cards in another family.
• If the first player does not receive a card, he or she picks from the pile. If the child draws an animal in the family he or she was trying for, then the child asks any player again for a chosen animal family member. If the right family card is not picked from the pile, the child adds the card to his or her hand and the next player takes a turn.

Note:
As the children make sets, they set them down. The child who has the most sets is the winner.

Option:
Make two copies of each card. Let children play Concentration.

Amazing Animals! © 1998 Monday Morning Books, Inc.

Animal Playing Cards

Lion	**Tiger**	**Leopard**
Cat Family	Cat Family	Cat Family
Badger	**Weasel**	**Skunk**
Weasel Family	Weasel Family	Weasel Family
Hippopotamus	**Pig**	**Peccary**
Pig Family	Pig Family	Pig Family
Camel	**Llama**	**Vicuna**
Camel Family	Camel Family	Camel Family

Animal Playing Cards

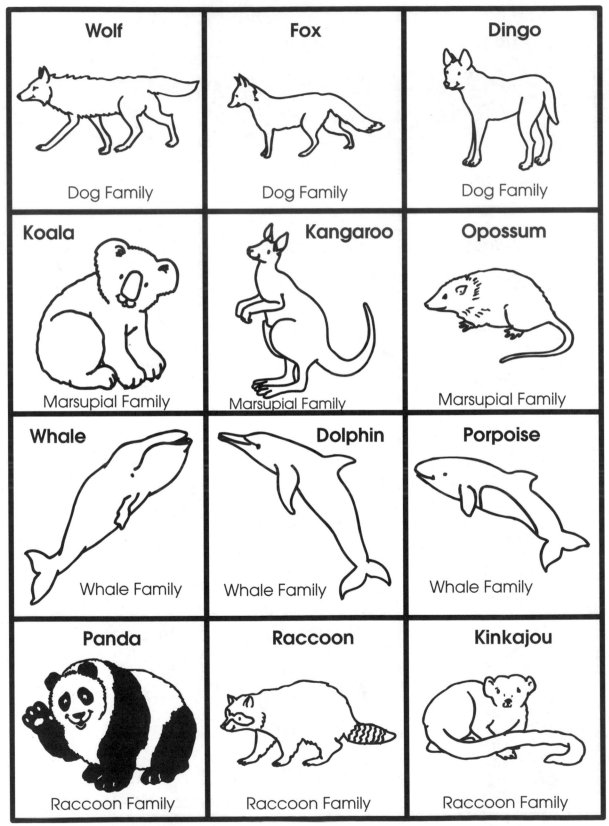

Wolf	Fox	Dingo
Dog Family	Dog Family	Dog Family

Koala	Kangaroo	Opossum
Marsupial Family	Marsupial Family	Marsupial Family

Whale	Dolphin	Porpoise
Whale Family	Whale Family	Whale Family

Panda	Raccoon	Kinkajou
Raccoon Family	Raccoon Family	Raccoon Family

Animal Playing Cards

| Gorilla | Chimp | Orangutan |
| Ape Family | Ape Family | Ape Family |

| Rabbit | Hare | Pika |
| Rabbit Family | Rabbit Family | Rabbit Family |

| Sheep | Goat | Ibex |
| Goat Family | Goat Family | Goat Family |

| Horse | Donkey | Zebra |
| Horse Family | Horse Family | Horse Family |

Group Animal Mural

Once children have learned about animal families, teach them the names of the various animal "groups."

Materials:
"Group Animal Chant" (p. 23), "Animal Playing Cards" (pp. 19-21), crayons or markers, scissors, butcher paper, glue or tape, decorative items (felt, fake fur, glitter, leaves or twigs, feathers)

Directions:
1. Duplicate the "Group Animal Chant" for each child.
2. Explain that groups of animals have special names. Read the chant with the children.
3. Duplicate and enlarge multiple copies of the "Animal Playing Cards" for children to color and cut out.
4. Have children work together to make a mural. They can either use the "Animal Playing Cards" or draw the animals themselves.
5. Children can decorate the animals with art materials.
6. Have the children post their animals on a large sheet of butcher paper. Children should group the same animals together.
7. Help the children label the groups. If a group name is not listed, they can name it based on another animal in its family (for example, a seal group is called a pod, so a walrus group could be called a pod). Or children can brainstorm names for the unnamed groups, for example, a valet of vicuña or a pocketful of pandas.

Options:
• Hold a contest to see who can come up with the best name for a group of kinkajous. Have children write their suggestions on slips of paper and vote for the favorite name.
• Have children discuss possible reasons behind the group names and record their suggested reasons in a class book.
• Divide the mural into habitats and provide tempera paint for children to use to paint the backgrounds. Post the animals in the correct habitats.
• Have each child find out a fact about an animal and write it on the back of the pattern. Post the animals using hinges of tape so people can read the facts on the backs.
• Post the Group Animal Chant in the center of the mural.

Amazing Animals! © 1998 Monday Morning Books, Inc.

Group Animal Chant

A band of gorillas plays under the trees
Near a drove of pigs and a swarm of bees.
A gam of whales and a pod of seals
Dance in the water with a spring of teals.
There's a group of teachers and a mom, or two,
But what do you call a bunch of kinkajous?

A cete of badgers and a pride of lions
Bake in the sun near a drift of swine.
A team of horses and a stud of mares
Are near a gang of elks and a husk of hares.
There's a group of parents and a child, or two,
But what do you call a bunch of kinkajous?

A murder of crows and a volery of birds
View the head of elephants and the camel herd.
A bed of clams and a monkey troop
Watch a leap of leopards and a covert of coots.
There's a group of kids and a dad, or two,
But what do you call a bunch of kinkajous?

A pack of wolves and a trip of goats
Observe the leap-frog games of a knot of toads.
A clowder of cats and a cry of quails
Befriend a colony of rabbits and a watch of nightingales.
There's a group of teenagers and a cousin, or two,
But what do you call a bunch of kinkajous?

There's a leash of foxes and a troop of kangaroos,
And a little group of chicks that we call a brood.
There's a rafter of turkeys and a skein of geese,
A horde of gnats and a flock of sheep,
A muster of peacocks and a pack of mules,
But this I don't know, so I'll ask you. . .
What do you call a bunch of kinkajous?

Amazing Animals! © 1998 Monday Morning Books, Inc.

Animal Glossaries

Materials:
"Animal Glossary" Hands-on Handouts (pp. 25-26), writing paper, pens or pencils, dictionaries, construction paper, stapler, glue, scissors

Directions:
1. Duplicate the glossary pages, making one set for each child. Explain that a glossary is a list of words with definitions.
2. Have children look up each word in the dictionary.
3. Children should write the definition next to the word to create their own animal glossaries. (Younger children can draw pictures.)
4. As children learn new animal words, have them add the words to their animal glossaries.
5. Provide construction paper and a stapler for children to use to bind their pages together. They can decorate the covers with pictures of animals.

Option:
White-out the words in the animal paw prints and duplicate one page for each child. Have children write in their own animal-related words and definitions.

Amazing Animals! © 1998 Monday Morning Books, Inc.

Animal Glossary

camouflage _____

fur _____

herbivore _____

hibernate _____

insectivore _____

Animal Glossary

marsupial

omnivore

quill

rodent

wool

Animal Spelling

Materials:
"Spelling Dot Patterns" (pp. 28-29), "Leopard Pattern" (p. 30), scissors, crayons or markers, tape or glue

Directions:
1. Duplicate the "Spelling Dot Patterns," making one sheet of each for each child and a few extra sheets for adult use.
2. Enlarge the "Leopard Pattern," color, and post on the bulletin board. Cut out one extra set of "dots" and post them on the "Leopard Pattern."
3. Have children learn how to spell each word. They can pair off and test each other as a way of practicing.
4. Host an "Animal Spelling" contest in your classroom. Keep one set of dots in a hat and pull out one at a time, asking each child in turn to spell the word on the dot.
5. Continue with the spelling contest, using the process of elimination. (Children who misspell a word sit down. The rest continue to try to spell the words.)

Note:
For additional spelling words, refer to the "Animal A to Z List" (p. 78).

Options:
• Duplicate blank spelling dots, and let children write in their own animal-related words.
• Duplicate both the "Leopard Pattern" and the dots for younger children. They can simply glue or tape the dots to the leopard and practice tracing the words.

Amazing Animals! © 1998 Monday Morning Books, Inc.

Spelling Dot Patterns

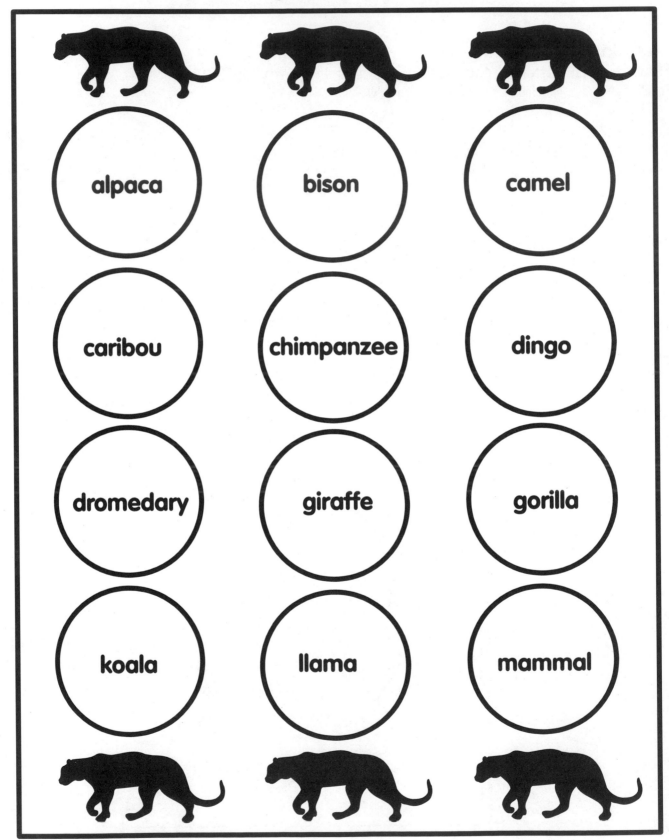

alpaca

bison

camel

caribou

chimpanzee

dingo

dromedary

giraffe

gorilla

koala

llama

mammal

Spelling Dot Patterns

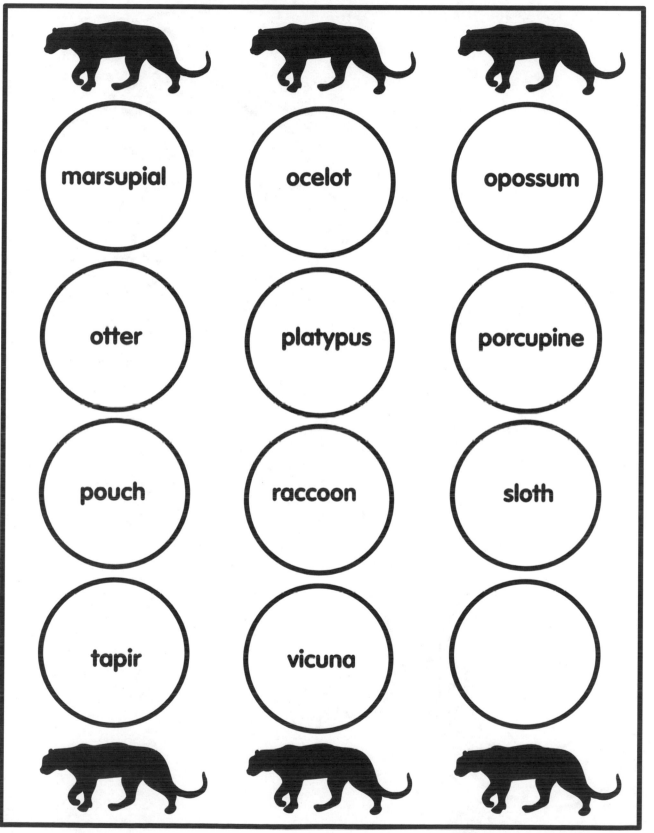

marsupial

ocelot

opossum

otter

platypus

porcupine

pouch

raccoon

sloth

tapir

vicuna

Leopard Pattern

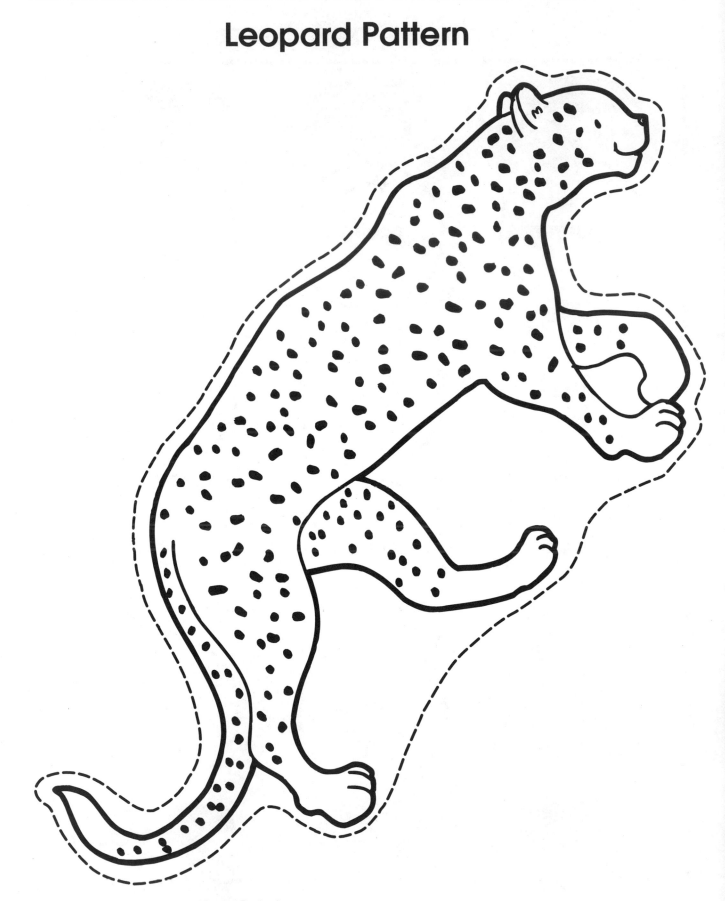

Interview an Animal

Materials:
"Super-Duper Fact Cards" (pp. 70-77), "Animal Fact Sheet"
Hands-on Handout (p. 32), "Animal Interview Sheet"
Hands-on Handout (p. 33), pencils or markers

Directions:
1. In these reports, children research animals and then play the part of their chosen animals in interview settings.
2. Let each child choose an animal from the "Super-Duper Fact Cards." Children can use the Fact Cards to research their topics. Or they can use books from the library.
3. Duplicate one copy of the "Animal Fact Sheet" Hands-on Handout and the "Animal Interview Sheet" Hands-on Handout for each child.
4. Have the children research their chosen animals using the guidelines on the "Animal Fact Sheet." Then have them write questions based on the facts using the "Animal Interview Sheet."
5. Once the children have finished their research, divide them into pairs. Have each partner take a turn interviewing the other in front of the class.
6. Set up an interview schedule, perhaps working through five to six interviews per day.

Note:
Children can also write reports on other animal-related topics. Have them choose from the "Animal A to Z List" (p. 78).

Options:
• Interviewers can hold simple microphones (cardboard tubes with egg carton sections or Styrofoam balls glued to the top).
• Interviewees can make simple costumes or masks to wear when they give their interviews.

Amazing Animals! © 1998 Monday Morning Books, Inc.

Animal Fact Sheet

Use this fact sheet to record at least four facts about your chosen animal. Remember to list the books you use. You can use the back of this sheet if you need more room.

My name is:

_____

My animal is:

_____

Fact:

_____

Fact:

_____

Fact:

_____

Fact:

_____

Books I used:

_____

Title:

_____

Author:

_____

Title:

_____

Author:

_____

Amazing Animals! © 1998 Monday Morning Books, Inc.

Animal Interview Sheet

Write your answers under the questions. Write your own question for question 5. Your partner will use these questions to interview you in front of the class.

Question 1: What type of animal are you?

_____

_____

Question 2: Where do you live?

_____

_____

Question 3: What types of foods do you eat?
(Are you an herbivore, carnivore, or omnivore?)

_____

_____

Question 4: What enemies do you have?

_____

_____

Question 5: _____

_____

_____

_____

Amazing Animals! © 1998 Monday Morning Books, Inc.

Pouch Facts

Materials:
"Marsupial Mamas" (p. 35), "Marsupial Babies" (p. 36), sturdy paper, "Super-Duper Fact Cards" on marsupials (kangaroos, p. 73; koalas, p. 73; opossums, p. 75), construction paper, crayons or markers, pens or pencils, scissors, tape or glue, small envelopes (optional)

Directions:
1. Duplicate and enlarge a copy of the "Marsupial Mamas" and "Marsupial Babies."
2. Trace the patterns onto sturdy paper and cut out. Make several for children to use as templates. Label each marsupial.
3. Let children choose which marsupials they want to research. Each child can trace a mama and baby animal onto construction paper and cut out. (Children who report on other marsupials can draw their own pictures.)
4. Have each child find one fact about the chosen animals using the Fact Cards or books found in the "Nonfiction Resources."
5. Have each child write a fact on a baby marsupial pattern.
6. Children can attach the opossum babies and koala babies to the backs of the mamas. For the kangaroos, they can make paper pouches to attach to the mama kangaroos or they can glue on envelope "pouches." The joeys can ride in the mamas' pouches.
7. Post the marsupials on a "Let's Find Out About Marsupials" bulletin board. Invite children to read the facts on each baby.

Options:
• Children can decorate the bulletin board to look like the habitats of their animals.
• Children can study other marsupials, including the spotted cuscus and the Tasmanian wolf.

Fun Fact:
The banded anteater, or "numbat," doesn't have a pouch. The tiny babies cling to the mother's long stomach hair.

Marsupial Mamas

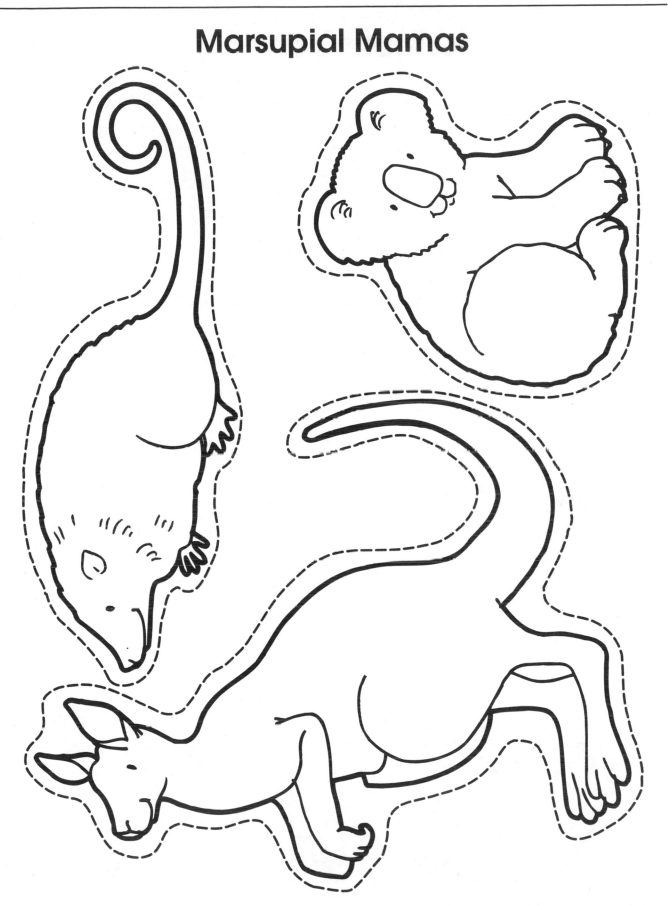

Marsupial Babies

Egg-Laying Mammals

Almost all mammals give birth to live young. The exceptions are the platypus and the spiny anteater. Both of these animals lay eggs. In this report, children research the platypus and the echidna (or spiny anteater) and write reports about these interesting mammals.

Materials:
"Platypus and Echidna Patterns" (p. 38), "Super-Duper Fact Cards" on the echidna (p. 71) and the platypus (p. 76), crayons or markers, scissors, white paper, pencils, felt or fake fur, toothpicks or pipe cleaners, glue, plastic eggs (available around Easter or at crafts stores), two baskets

Directions:
1. Divide the children into pairs.
2. Duplicate the "Platypus and Echidna Patterns" and cut them out. Make enough copies for each team to have one.
3. Have each team choose one animal to research using the "Super-Duper Fact Cards" or books from the "Nonfiction Resources."
4. Children can decorate the patterns. Provide fake fur or felt for teams to use to decorate the platypuses and toothpicks or pipe cleaners for children to glue to the echidnas.
5. Give each team one plastic egg and have the teams write one important fact about their chosen creature and place it in the egg.
6. Post the platypus pictures on one bulletin board and the echidnas on another. Place the baskets beneath the pictures. Place the correct eggs in the baskets.
7. Invite students to take out the eggs one at a time and read the facts that are inside.

Option:
If plastic eggs are not available, have children write the facts on egg-shaped cards.

Amazing Animals! © 1998 Monday Morning Books, Inc.

Platypus and Echidna Patterns

Apartment Sloths

Sloths spend almost all of their time hanging upside down from trees. They have curved claws, like hooks, to cling with. Sloths have coarse fur and short snouts. Tiny creatures, such as moths and mites, burrow in the sloth's fur, making the sloths their homes.

Materials:
"Sloth and Friends Patterns" (p. 40), "Super-Duper Fact Card" on sloths (p. 77), crayons or markers, scissors, butcher paper, glue, pens or pencils, twigs and leaves (optional)

Directions:
1. Duplicate the "Sloth and Friends Patterns" for each child to color and cut out.
2. Provide copies of the "Super-Duper Fact Card" on sloths, or other sloth resources for children to use.
3. Have children research sloths.
4. Children can write one or more facts about the sloth on the sloth patterns.
5. Have children glue the "friends" to the sloths.
6. Post the sloths on a "Super Sloth" bulletin board. Children can add twigs or leaves to help hide the sloths in the trees.

Fun Fact:
The sloth can turn its head 270 degrees so it can look at things right-side up when it's upside down.

Amazing Animals! © 1998 Monday Morning Books, Inc.

Sloth and Friends Patterns

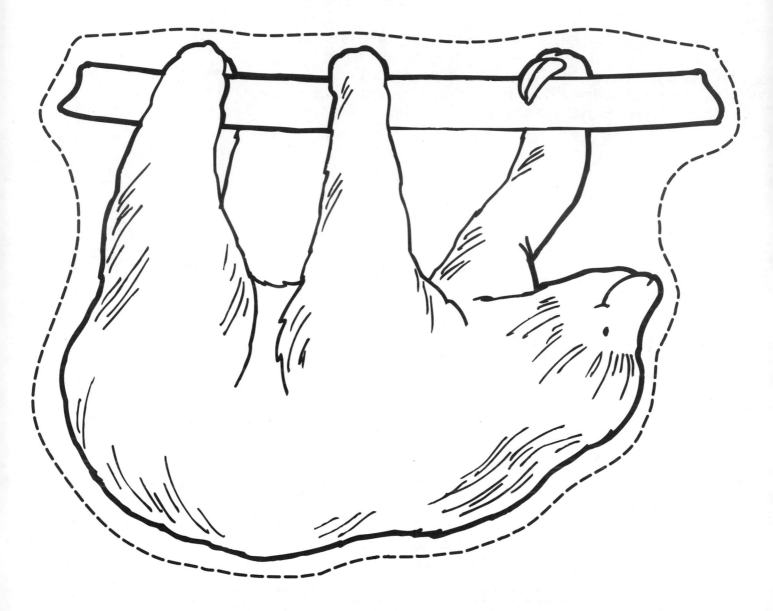

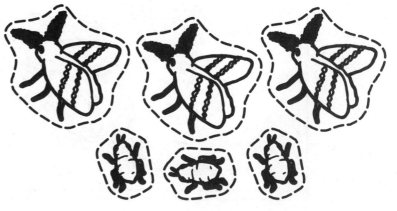

"Talking" Like Animals

Koko the gorilla learned to speak in sign language. In the wild, animals have many different ways of communicating with each other. They need to be able to warn each other of danger, to find mates, to recognize their babies, and to ward off enemies.

Materials:
"'Talking' Like Animals" Hands-on Handout (p. 42), "Oral Report Sheet" Hands-on Handout (p. 43), pens or pencils

Directions:
1. Discuss the many different ways that people communicate with each other. Have children brainstorm a list together. (The list might include talking on the phone, faxing, speaking in person, using sign language, sending e-mail, whispering, singing, waving, using a video phone, and so on.)
2. Discuss the fact that animals must have different ways to communicate.
3. Let children choose animals to research, using the "'Talking' Like Animals" Hands-on Handout. They can use the "Super-Duper Fact Cards" at the end of this book, or they can use library books for researching.
4. Have children give short (one- to two-minute) oral reports in which they each discuss their chosen animal's methods of communicating. They might also give examples of the way their animals give and receive information. Children can prepare for their oral reports using the guidelines on the "Oral Report Sheet."

Options:
• Children can demonstrate the sounds of their chosen animal.
• Speakers can give the rest of the class a chance to "talk" like the chosen animal. For example, if a child researched a panda, he or she can teach the class a few chirps.
• Read *Koko's Kitten* by Dr. Francine Patterson (Scholastic, 1985) to learn more about Koko, the amazing gorilla.

"Talking" Like Animals

Animals "talk" to each other in different ways:

- Elephants greet each other by touching trunks.

- Fur seals roar, stare sideways at their opponents, or lunge to settle arguments.

- Baby fur seals bleat right after birth. Their mothers know them by their smell and by the sound of their bleats.

- Snow leopards purr instead of roar. Their purr means "Stay away!"

- Pandas are usually quiet, but when they seek out another panda they growl, honk, and even chirp!

- To scare off enemies, gorillas beat their chests, roar, and charge.

- When a zebra is scared it makes a loud braying noise that ends in a whinny.

Oral Report Sheet

Answer the following questions that relate to your animal:

• My animal's name is:

_____

• My animal "talks" by:

_____

_____

• If my animal is in danger, it does this:

_____

_____

_____

_____

_____

• Draw a picture of your animal, or trace one from a book. Show this picture during your report.

Animal Nicknames

Orangutans have been called "hairy red men of the woods"; bats are sometimes known as "creatures of the night"; lions are called "the kings of the jungle"; manatees have been named "sea cows"; and camels have been called "ships of the desert."

Materials:
Drawing paper, crayons or markers, pens or pencils

Directions:
1. Have children brainstorm reasons why a hippopotamus might be called a "river horse."
2. Discuss other animals that have descriptive nicknames (listed above).
3. Have children brainstorm descriptive names for animals they've studied. For example, meerkats always post a sentry when they're foraging. Standing tall, the sentry looks like a "watch cat." Or have children choose animals to research and then come up with descriptive nicknames based on facts they learn.
4. Each child can draw a picture of his or her chosen animal and write the nickname below it.
5. Post the completed pictures on a bulletin board, or bind them in a classroom "Nickname Book."

Option:
Have children invent nicknames for themselves that describe something they're good at.

Elephant Report

Materials:
"Elephant Pattern" (p. 46), "Super-Duper Fact Card" on elephants (p. 71), scissors, pens or pencils, gray paper

Directions:
1. Duplicate a copy of the "Elephant Pattern" onto gray paper for each child to cut out.
2. Have children research elephants using the "Super-Duper Fact Card," or other resource materials.
3. Have the children write their favorite facts on the front of the elephant patterns.
4. Post the completed elephant reports on a bulletin board, linking the elephant patterns together from trunk to tail.

Options:
• Duplicate the elephant patterns onto white paper and let children color the patterns using gray crayons.
• Let children create a mural background for their elephants. Have children research the elephants' habitats and then paint a butcher paper mural accordingly. They can divide the paper in two and draw the habitat of the Indian elephant on one side and the habitat of the African elephant on the other.
• Some people believe elephants are related to the tiny hyrax. Have children look up this little animal and brainstorm possible connections.

Amazing Animals! © 1998 Monday Morning Books, Inc.

Elephant Pattern

Animal Newspaper

Materials:
"Newspaper Project" Hands-on Handout (p. 48), "Newspaper Pattern" (p. 49), "Animal Playing Cards" (pp. 19-21), crayons or markers, animal patterns from other activities, scissors, glue

Directions:
1. Duplicate a copy of the "Newspaper Project" Hands-on Handout and the "Newspaper Pattern" for each child.
2. Have each child choose an animal, or family of animals, to feature in a newspaper.
3. Children can use their previously written animal reports to write short stories about the animals.
4. Provide "Animal Playing Cards" patterns, or animal patterns from the various activities throughout the book, for children to use to illustrate their newspapers. They can cut out the patterns and glue them in the "photo" box. Or they can draw their own versions.
5. Help children come up with headlines for their stories and names for their papers. You might bring in the front section from a local newspaper for children to look at. Newspapers often have similar names, for example, Tribune, Chronicle, Times, Post. Children could name their papers according to the stories featured, for example, "The Orangutan Post" or the "Vicuña Tribune."
6. Bind the finished papers together in a class book.

Options:
• Children can work in groups to create larger papers.
• Explain that news stories generally cover the five w's: who, what, when, where, and why. Have children try to answer these questions in their stories. For example, if a child's paper featured elephants, the *who* would be "elephants," *what* might be "being killed for their tusks," *when* might be "now," *where* could be "in Africa," and the *why* could be "for money."
• Have children write interviews for their papers. They can use the interviews they did for the class (p. 31). Or they might do a class on-line interview, or interview a guest speaker. Consider inviting your school librarian, a representative from the local animal shelter, a museum curator, or a local zoo keeper to take part in this activity.

Amazing Animals! © 1998 Monday Morning Books, Inc.

Newspaper Project

What You Do:

1. Choose an animal to research. Write the name of your animal here:

2. Research your animal and write down three facts about it. These might include its habitat (where it lives), its diet (what it eats), and its enemies (which creatures it tries to avoid).

a)

_____

b)

_____

c)

_____

3. Brainstorm what you want to write about your animal. For example, if it has an enemy, you might write a story about how it protects itself. (Is it a fast runner? Does it use camouflage?) If it's endangered, you might write why people have hunted it. (Do people use its fur for coats or its tusks for jewelry?) Does your animal do something special? (Can it locate its food by sound? Does it change color in the winter?) Use the back of this paper for your brainstorming.

4. Use your facts and brainstorming ideas to write a short news story about your animal. First, write a draft. Then copy the story on the newspaper pattern.

5. Illustrate your story with patterns or by drawing a picture of your chosen animal.

Newspaper Pattern

If You Give A Mouse a Cookie

Story:

If You Give a Mouse a Cookie by Laura Joffe Numeroff, illustrated by Felicia Bond (HarperCollins, 1985).
This clever children's book is already a classic! It explains exactly what chain of events will follow if you invite a mouse into your home for a cookie. The sequel to this story, *If You Give a Moose a Muffin*, is equally delightful.

Setting the Stage:

• Collect menus (or photocopies of menus) from various local restaurants and post them on a bulletin board.
• Bring in a label from a can of pet food or the ingredients list from a bag of pet food.
• If you have a classroom pet, have children observe the animal when it eats.
• Have a classroom potluck, with every child bringing in something from home to share.
• Post a food pyramid in the classroom. Discuss varied diets and have children help create a diet that includes foods from all of the groups.

Tricky Tongue Twister:

• *An ocelot can eat a lot.*

If You Give a Bat a Mango

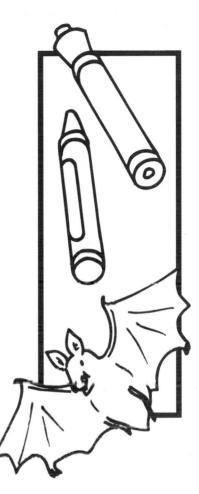

Materials:
"Wild Kingdom Menu" Hands-on Handout (p. 52),
"Super-Duper Fact Cards" (pp. 70-77), drawing paper,
crayons or markers, pens or pencils

Directions:
1. After reading *If You Give a Mouse a Cookie*, explain that
students will be making book covers for their own storybooks.
2. *If You Give a Mouse a Cookie* is a fictional account of
what mice eat. In reality, mice nibble seeds, grains, and
some plants. Pet mice like to eat lettuce, celery, carrots,
and birdseed.
3. Have each child choose an animal to research.
4. Duplicate copies of the "Wild Kingdom Menu" for children
to use to research what types of food their chosen animals
eat. (Children can also use the "Super-Duper Fact Cards" or
other resources.)
5. Have children write a title for a make-believe book,
following the style of *If You Give a Mouse a Cookie*, but
using real foods that animals eat.
6. Provide art materials for children to use to decorate their
covers.
7. Post the finished book covers on an "If You Give..."
bulletin board.

Note:
The diets listed on the "Wild Kingdom Menu" are mostly for
fruit- and insect-eaters. If you want to avoid such book titles
as *If You Give a Lion a Zebra*, make a rule that children write
covers only for herbivores and insectivores.

Option:
Children can write and illustrate picture books that go
with the covers.

Amazing Animals! © 1998 Monday Morning Books, Inc.

Wild Kingdom Menu

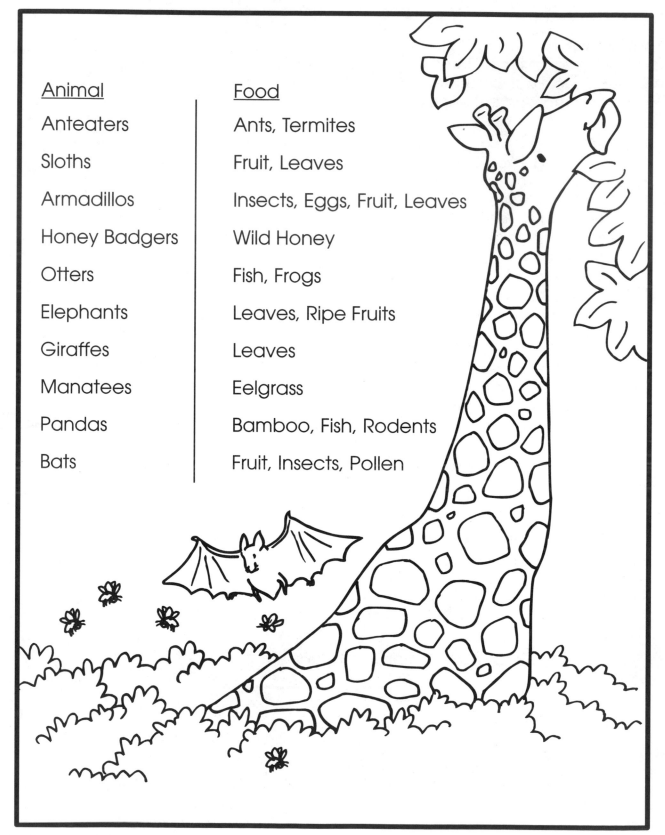

Animal	Food
Anteaters	Ants, Termites
Sloths	Fruit, Leaves
Armadillos	Insects, Eggs, Fruit, Leaves
Honey Badgers	Wild Honey
Otters	Fish, Frogs
Elephants	Leaves, Ripe Fruits
Giraffes	Leaves
Manatees	Eelgrass
Pandas	Bamboo, Fish, Rodents
Bats	Fruit, Insects, Pollen

Pamela Camel

Story:

Pamela Camel by Bill Peet (Houghton Mifflin, 1984). Pamela the camel lives in a circus and is tired of being called "stupid." She runs away to prove everyone wrong. On her first day of freedom, she discovers a break on a railroad track. Her courageous manner of warning the train engineer wins her much praise.

Setting the Stage:

• Decorate the classroom in a circus theme. Bring in colored crepe paper to hang from the bulletin board. Cut colored construction paper circles to post as balloons around the room.
• Make popcorn for a snack.
• Read other circus books with the children.
• Have children do research to find out which type of camel Pamela is: Bactrian or Arabian. (She has one hump, which means she's an Arabian.)
• Use the newspaper pattern (p. 49) to let children make other headlines like the one in the book: "Camel Saves Express Train." Have children think of other ways to get the same point across, for example, "Brave Camel Warns of Danger."

Tongue Twister:

• *Riding a camel's hump is bumpy.*

Camel Caravan Stories

Camels have been called "Ships of the Desert" because they can go six to eight days without water in the summer. During the winter, they can go longer than six weeks without a drink! Camels have wide, padded feet that keep them from sinking into the sand. Their long eyelashes keep sand out of their eyes and they can close their nostrils, too! Camels store fat in their humps. If they cannot eat regularly, they turn the fat into food.

Materials:
"Camel Patterns" (p. 55), "Super-Duper Fact Card" on camels (p. 70), crayons or markers, scissors

Directions:
1. Divide the class into groups of four.
2. Have the children work together to write a short (one page) story about a camel or a group of camels. They can use the "Super-Duper Fact Card" for research, or they can use other resources. Encourage children to write fictional stories that include some facts.
3. Copy the "Camel Patterns." Give each group four camels.
4. Have the children divide their story into four parts and have each child write one part on a camel.
5. Post the completed camel stories in the correct order on a "Camel Caravan" bulletin board.

Note:
Children can retell a familiar tale or song using camels as the main characters. For example, they could write stories about: Goldilocks and the Three Camels, The Three Camels Gruff, The Three Little Camels, The Boy Who Cried "Camel," I Know an Old Lady Who Swallowed a Camel, and so on. They can write the stories to include camel facts or to make the stories work with camel characters. (The camels in "Goldilocks" would eat plants instead of porridge. In "The Three Camels Gruff," camels, instead of billy goats, would cross the bridge over the troll.)

Option:
Work together to write a class camel story. Have each child write a line of the story on a camel pattern, and post the entire story along one wall.

Amazing Animals! © 1998 Monday Morning Books, Inc.

Camel Patterns

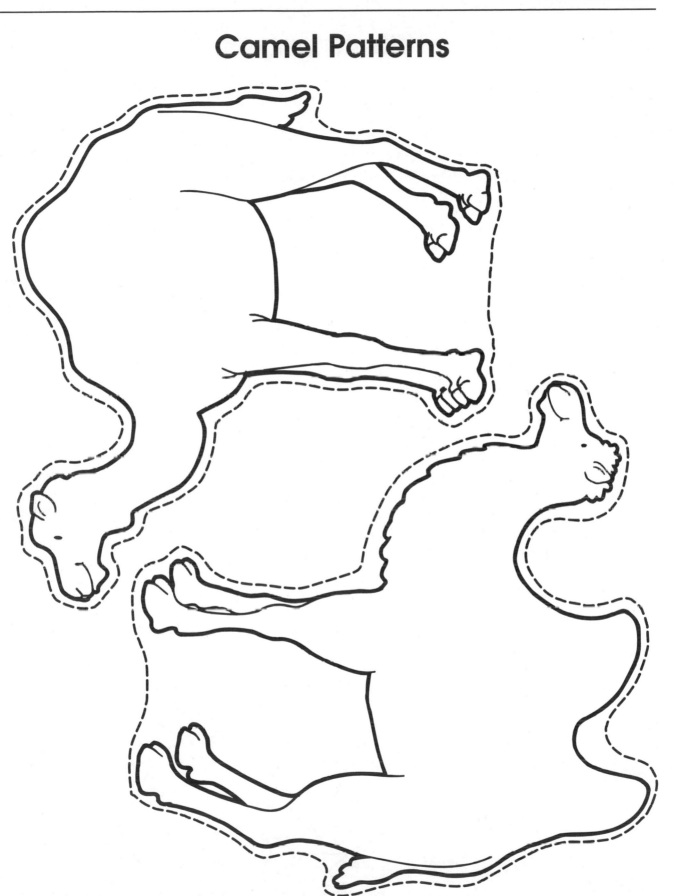

Stellaluna

Story:

Stellaluna by Janell Cannon (Harcourt Brace, 1993). A baby bat named Stellaluna is separated from her mother and raised by a bird family. Although Stellaluna tries her best, she is unable to do the same things as the baby birds. Finally, she is reunited with her mother and taught that she does everything exactly the way bats are supposed to! (This book includes two pages of bat facts at the back.) *Stellaluna* is available on audiotape from High Windy Audio.

Setting the Stage:

• Stellaluna is a fruit bat. Serve mango slices or other types of fruit as a snack.
• Stellaluna tries to like insects, but she doesn't! Some people eat insects. Make an insect snack found in the Food Insects Newsletter for children to try. Write to: Professor DeFoliart, c/o the Department of Entomology, 545 Russell Laboratories, University of Wisconsin, Madison, WI 53706. The newsletter is published three times a year, and a donation of at least $5.00 is requested to defray printing costs.
• Most bats sleep during the day. They hang upside down in trees and caves. Hang the bats (p. 8) upside down from different pieces of clothesline strung across the room. Dim the lights and have children pretend they are in a bat cave.
• Bring in a bat house for children to observe.
• Teach children the Mother Goose rhyme about bats, listed below:

> *Bat, bat, come under my hat,*
> *And I'll give you a slice of bacon;*
> *And when I bake, I'll give you a cake,*
> *If I am not mistaken.*

Tongue Twisters:

• *The bratty bats drive Barbara batty.*
• *Bats in the cave try hard to behave.*

Mama and Baby Match

In *Stellaluna*, the mama and baby bat are separated. When they are finally reunited, both are very happy to see each other. The mama smells the baby and knows that it truly is her long lost daughter. In this activity, children unite mama and baby animals.

Materials:
"Mama Animals" (p. 58), "Baby Animals" (p. 59), crayons or markers, scissors

Directions:
1. Duplicate the "Mama Animals" and "Baby Animals."
2. Color the patterns, cut apart, laminate, and cut them apart again. Make sure to leave a thin laminate border to prevent peeling.
3. Have children match the patterns together in a Concentration game. All of the patterns are shuffled and spread face down. Children take turns flipping over two cards at a time. If the cards are a mama and baby of the same animal, the child takes the cards and turns two more over. If the cards don't match, they are turned back over and the next child takes a turn.

Option:
Have children learn about how mama and baby animals locate each other, for example, seals learn their babies' smells and sounds. Create a bulletin board of facts and pictures showing mamas and babies together.

Mama Animals

Baby Animals

The Tortoise and the Hare

Story:
The Tortoise and the Hare: An Aesop Fable adapted and illustrated by Janet Stevens (Holiday House, 1984).
In this famous fable, an obnoxious hare challenges the slow and steady turtle to a race. Although he doesn't think he can win, the tortoise finally accepts the hare's challenge. On the day of the race, the hare sprints far ahead of tortoise, and then decides to relax for awhile. The tortoise marches onward while the hare naps and dreams of winning. At the end, the tortoise's hard work and perseverance beat the bragging hare!

Setting the Stage:
• Have a short foot race. Serve lemonade at the finish line.
• Act out the story with one child playing the tortoise and another playing the hare. Let children take turns with the different parts.
• Tell and act out other famous fables from Aesop.
• When you read the fables, gather the children around you and tell the story in the manner of an old-fashioned storyteller. (Learn the story by heart and tell it without the book.)
• Let children take turns telling fables that they know.

Other Aesop's Fables:
• *Aesop's Fables* adapted by Louis Untermeyer (Golden Press, 1965).
• *Tales from Aesop* retold by Harold Jones (Watts, 1982).
• *Twelve Tales from Aesop* illustrated by Eric Carle (Putnam's, 1980).

Tongue Twister:
• *Turtles slowly cross the hurdles.*

Aesop's Bar Graph

Materials:
"Bar Graph Pattern" (p. 62), crayons or markers

Directions:
1. Discuss each of the stories listed on the bar graph and their morals (see sidebar on right). See if the children understand and agree with the statements.
2. Have children share experiences of their own that fit the messages or morals taught in various Aesop's tales. For example, has a child ever plodded through a difficult project from start to finish, like the tortoise in "The Tortoise and the Hare"? Has a child ever come to someone's surprise aid, as in "The Lion and the Mouse"?
3. Create a classroom graph of experiences that fall under different headings. Duplicate and enlarge the graph on the following page, or make a transparency for an overhead projector. Or make your own graph, letting the children help you choose the fables and the morals.
4. Give each child a turn to color in the squares of the graph that represent personal experiences.
5. Post the completed bar graph in the classroom where children can add to it as they desire.

Option:
Make a classroom bar graph using retold fables the children create (pp. 63-64). On this graph, the stories may have new titles, such as "The Jaguar and the Sloth," but would most likely have the same morals as Aesop's "The Tortoise and the Hare."

Title: "The Tortoise and the Hare"
Moral: Slow and Steady Wins the Race

Title: "The Lion and the Mouse"
Moral: The Smallest May Help the Greatest

Title: "The Wolf and the Fox"
Moral: Actions Speak Louder than Tears

Title: "The Bear and the Two Travellers"
Moral: Choose Your Friends Wisely

Title: "The Fox and the Grapes"
Moral: Be Satisfied with What You Have

Once I felt like the tortoise.

Bar Graph Pattern

	The Tortoise and the Hare	The Lion and the Mouse	The Fox and the Grapes	The Bear and the Two Travellers	The Wolf and the Fox
30					
29					
28					
27					
26					
25					
24					
23					
22					
21					
20					
19					
18					
17					
16					
15					
14					
13					
12					
11					
10					
9					
8					
7					
6					
5					
4					
3					
2					
1					

Writing an Animal Fable

Materials:
"Animal Fables" Hands-on Handout (p. 64), drawing and writing paper, crayons or markers, pens or pencils

Directions:
1. After reading several of Aesop's fables, have children choose their favorite.
2. Duplicate the "Animal Fables" Hands-on Handout for each child.
3. Children can retell the Aesop's tales using animals they've studied in class. For example, the story of "The Tortoise and the Hare" could be retold using another slow animal and another speedy animal: "The Sloth and the Jaguar."
4. Children can add facts that they've learned to their stories, for example, they might set the tales in the correct habitats of their animals.
5. Have children write and illustrate the retold tales. Younger children can dictate their stories.

Note:
If children have a difficult time thinking of a new tale, they could choose to write one from the list below:

Aesop's Fables
- "The Camel at First Sight"
- "The Boy Who Cried Wolf"
- "The Sow and the Wolf"
- "The Leopard and the Fox"

Retold Fables:
- "The Vicuña at First Sight"
- "The Boy Who Cried Dingo"
- "The Peccary and the Lion"
- "The Okapi and the Coyote"

Amazing Animals! © 1998 Monday Morning Books, Inc.

Animal Fables

What You Do:
1. Choose a fable that you know and like.
2. Choose an animal (or animals) to replace the animal (or animals) in the original story.
3. In your own words, retell the fable replacing the original animal with your new animal.
4. Create a new title for your story. For example, if you retold the story of the "Lion and the Mouse" with a tiger and a shrew, your title could simply be "The Tiger and the Shrew."
5. Draw a picture to fit what happens in your story. You might draw several different pictures to show the different events.

Amazing Animals! © 1998 Monday Morning Books, Inc.

Amazing Animals Program

Songs:
- "Oh, My Darling, Porcupine"
- "An Ocelot Roams"
- "We Swing from the Trees"
- "Baby Animal Chant"
- "Kangaroos, Elephants, Manatees, and Whales"

Featuring:

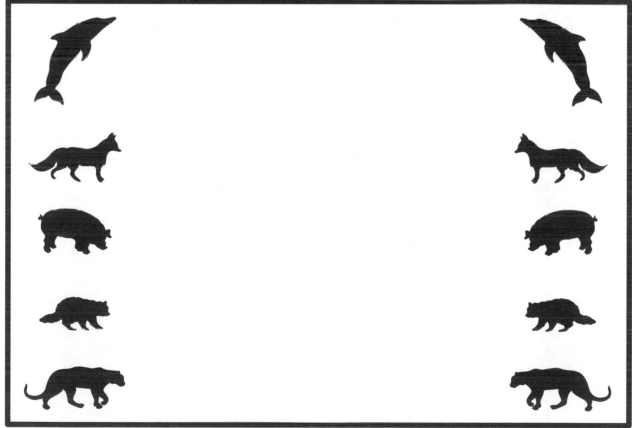

Oh, My Darling, Porcupine

(to the tune of "Oh, My Darling, Clementine")

Oh, my darling,
Oh, my darling,
Oh, my darling, Porcupine.
You have quills that make you prickly,
Up and down your soft, brown spine.

You're a prickly, little creature.
You can roll up like a bug.
Then your quills stick out all over,
And you're awfully hard to hug.

Oh, my darling,
Oh, my darling,
Oh, my darling, Porcupine.
You have quills that make you prickly,
Up and down your soft, brown spine.

Note: Make a simple costume from a brown paper bag. Tape pipe cleaners or straws along the back of the bag for quills.

Amazing Animals! © 1998 Monday Morning Books, Inc.

An Ocelot Roams

(to the tune of "Home on the Range")

An ocelot roams in its dark, forest home
And it prowls in the wild cat way.
It's yellow and brown, with black spots all around—
Blending in helps it search for its prey.

Stripes, rings, and black spots
Help the ocelots blend in a lot.
When they hunt through the trees,
They're disguised with such ease,
That sometimes you can't see ocelots.

Note: Paint a backdrop using black, brown, and yellow tempera paint. Use the same colors to make paper bag costumes. Add simple ears attached to headbands and draw on whiskers with makeup.

We Swing from the Trees

(to the tune of "Home on the Range")

We swing from the trees,
Just my brothers and me,
We have fun on a bright summer day.
We hang upside down,
Making noise like a clown,
Because that's the way chimpanzees play.

My home is a tree,
And I live there with my family.
We eat fruit by the bunch,
On bananas we munch,
Because that is the chimpanzee way.

Note: Each child can hold a banana during this song to use as a microphone. They can eat the bananas at the end of the performance.

Amazing Animals! © 1998 Monday Morning Books, Inc.

Baby Animal Chant

A baby dog is called a puppy.
A rhino is called a calf.
A skunk is called a kitten—
Now, isn't that a laugh?

A baby eel is called an elver.
A deer is called a fawn.
Have you ever seen a joey
Jump across the lawn?

A baby lion is a cub.
A bear is called one, too.
A goat is called a kid—
And, hey, so are you!

A baby cat is called a kitten.
An owl is an owlet.
Wild fowl are called flappers,
And an eagle is an eaglet.

Baby birds are called nestlings,
But partridges are cheepers.
Tigers are called whelps,
And mackerels are tinkers.

A baby duck is called a duckling.
A horse is called a colt.
A pig is called a suckling,
And a zebra is a foal.

A baby rabbit is a bunny.
A goose is called a gosling.
A pigeon is a squeaker,
And a cod is called a codling.

But what about the joey?
Well, I'll give you a clue:
It lives inside the pouch of a mama kangaroo!

Note: Let each child recite a different line from this poem.

Amazing Animals! © 1998 Monday Morning Books, Inc.

Kangaroos, Elephants, Manatees, and Whales

(to the tune of "Jingle Bells")

Kangaroos, elephants, manatees, and whales,
Angelfish and llamas, ostriches and snails.
They have one thing in common, now guess it if you can.
They all share planet Earth with an animal called man.

So let's all lend a hand,
And keep this planet safe.
We want to share our land
With each animal and race.

Now, take a look around,
And hold each other's hand.
Isn't that a pretty sound?
Peace rings across the land!

Oh, kangaroos, elephants, manatees, and whales,
Angelfish and llamas, ostriches and snails.
They have one thing in common, now guess it if you can.
They all share planet Earth with an animal called man.

Note: Children can make simple costumes from paper bags and tempera paint to wear during this song. Have all of the children hold hands during the chorus.

Bat Facts

Habitat: Bats can be found around the world, but prefer tropical regions.
Sleeping Habits: Most bats sleep during the day. They sleep upside down with their wings folded.
Food: Some bats eat fruit. Others eat insects. Others eat pollen.
Size: The largest bat has a wingspan of nearly 5 ft. (2 m.). The smallest bat is the bumblebee bat of Thailand with a wingspan of 6 in. (16 cm.).
Flight: Bats are the only mammals that can fly.
Super-Duper Fact: One species of bat has a tongue longer than its head and body combined!

Camel Facts

Types: Bactrian camels have two humps. Arabian camels have one.
Habitat: Arabian camels live in the Middle East and North Africa. Bactrians live in the Gobi Desert.
Food: Camels eat plants. They can go for six weeks or longer without water during cool weather. They get their water from moist plants.
Size: The Bactrian camel can stand 7 ft. (2.1 m.) to the top of its hump. It weighs about 1,200 lbs. (545.5 kg.). Arabians weigh the same but are about 6 in. (15.4 cm.) taller.
Super-Duper Fact: Dromedaries (a type of Arabian camel bred for riding) can gallop 100 miles (161.3 km.) in one day.

Echidna Facts

Habitat: Echidnas live in Australia and New Guinea.
Food: Echidnas eat earthworms, ants, and termites.
Babies: Echidnas are monotremes. These are types of mammals that lay eggs. Their eggs have leathery shells. The babies are only about .5 in. (1 cm.) long when they first hatch.
Name: Echidnas are also called spiny anteaters.
Way of Feeding: Echidnas do not have teeth. They catch their food with their long, sticky tongues.
Enemies: To avoid danger, they roll up into tight, spiky balls.
Super-Duper Fact: Echidnas can go for a month without food.

Elephant Facts

Habitat: African elephants live in tropical Africa. Indian elephants live In Southeast Asia.
Size: Indian elephants grow to 10 ft. (3 m.) tall and weigh 4.5 tons (4050 kg.). The African elephant is the largest living land mammal. It grows to 11 ft. (3.5 m.) tall and weighs up to 8 tons (7200 kg.).
Enemies: People kill elephants for their tusks.
Way of Feeding: Elephants grab food with their trunks. They use their trunks to drink water.
Food: Elephants eat leaves, branches, twigs, and ripe fruit.
Super-Duper Fact: Elephants grow new teeth five times.

Giraffe Facts

Habitat: Giraffes live in Africa.
Food: Giraffes feed on the green leaves of trees 20 hours a day.
Way of Feeding: A giraffe pulls leaves toward it with its sticky tongue.
Size: Giraffes are the tallest animals. They can grow to 18 ft. (6 m.) tall and can weigh 3,000 lbs. (1,350 kg.).
Babies: A month after a giraffe is born, it lives in a "nursery herd."
Enemies: Its height allows a giraffe to see its enemies coming.
Camouflage: Giraffes are yellow with dark brown spots. Their coats help them blend in with the trees.
Super-Duper Fact: Male giraffes fight with their skulls.

Hippopotamus Facts

Habitat: Hippos live in rivers and lakes in Africa.
Food: Hippos eat the tall grasses that grow on the river banks.
Babies: Hippo mothers teach their young good hippo manners!
Size: Hippos can weigh 3.5 tons (3150 kg.) and grow to 14 ft. (4.5 m.) long. Pygmy hippos are only about 5 ft. (1.5 m.) long.
Enemies: Large crocodiles are the hippo's main enemy.
Super-Duper Fact: The hippo's delicate skin must stay wet to keep from burning. It produces its own type of suntan lotion that oozes from its glands.

Amazing Animals! © 1998 Monday Morning Books, Inc.

Kangaroo Facts

Habitat: 52 kinds of kangaroos live in Australia and New Guinea.
Food: Kangaroos eat grass.
Babies: Baby kangaroos are called joeys.
Size: The largest kangaroo is the red kangaroo. It can be 6.5 ft. (2 m.) tall. The smallest is the rat-kangaroo, which is 20 in. (50 cm.) long.
Types: Some kangaroos are called wallabies and others are wallaroos.
Enemies: Dingoes, or wild dogs, eat kangaroos, so kangaroos must be on the lookout!
Super-Duper Fact: Kangaroos are marsupials. A marsupial mama carries her baby in a pouch.

Koala Facts

Habitat: Koalas live in Australia.
Food: Koalas eat only eucalyptus leaves. Of the hundreds of varieties of eucalyptus, koalas eat only 12. Koalas eat 2.25 lbs. (1 kg.) of eucalyptus leaves and shoots a day.
Size: Koalas grow to be 2 ft. (.6 m.) tall and weigh 33 lbs. (15 kg.).
Names: Other names for koalas include bangaroo, koolewong, karbor, and narnagoon.
Babies: Kangaroos are marsupials. A marsupial mama carries her baby in a pouch.
Super-Duper Fact: The eucalyptus koalas eat serves as a bug repellent. Bugs don't like the smell!

Amazing Animals! © 1998 Monday Morning Books, Inc.

Llama Facts

Habitat: Llamas live in South America.
Size: Adult llamas can weigh up to 400 lbs. (181 kg.) and stand 6 ft. (1.8 m.) tall at the head. Baby llamas weigh between 18 and 33 lbs. (8-15 kg.) at birth.
Food: Llamas eat grassy reeds, mosses, lichens, and low shrubs.
Relatives: They are related to camels, alpaca, guanaco, and vicuña.

Uses: Llamas are used to transport goods in places where cars can't go. Their wool is used to make sweaters and blankets.
Super-Duper Fact: Llamas can go for days without water and with little food.

Manatee Facts

Habitat: Manatees live in seas and rivers, in both fresh and salt water. Florida manatees are protected.
Food: Manatees eat sea grasses as well as plants floating on top of the water.
Way of Feeding: Manatees have flat noses, which allow them to feed on plants near the water's surface.
Size: They can grow from 8 to 14 ft. (2.5 to 4.5 m.) from head to tail and weigh up to 3,300 lbs. (1,500 kg.).

Babies: Manatees communicate with their babies by chirping.
Super-Duper Fact: Some people believe that sailors mistook manatees for mermaids.

Opossum Facts

Habitat: Opossums can be found in the United States.

Food: Opossums eat crayfish, snails, earthworms, frogs, salamanders, and other small animals.

Size: An adult male opossum can grow up to 40 in. (1 m.) in length.

Enemies: When the opossum is attacked, it pretends to be dead. (This is called "playing possum.")

Babies: Opossums are marsupials. This means that the females carry their babies in pouches.

Super-Duper Fact: The opossum has been around for millions of years. It shared the Earth with the dinosaurs!

Orangutan Facts

Habitat: Orangutans live in Borneo and the northern part of Sumatra. These two islands are between Asia and Australia.

Food: Orangutans eat fruit, leaves, bark, and insects.

Size: Females weigh 73 to 92 lbs. (33 to 42 kg.) and stand 42 to 47 in. (107 to 120 cm.) tall. Males weigh 176 to 200 lbs. (80 to 91 kg.) and stand 53 to 55 in. (136 to 141 cm.) tall.

Sleeping Habits: At night, orangutans build nests in trees.

Super-Duper Fact: Male orangutans have large flat cheeks and long red beards and mustaches.

Panda Facts

Habitat: Pandas live in China.
Size: A full-grown giant panda can be 6 ft. (1.8 m.) long from its head to its tail.
Food: Pandas eat bamboo plants, flowers, fish, birds, small animals, and sometimes honey.
Babies: Baby pandas are very tiny. They weigh about as much as an apple.
Families: Pandas live by themselves. A baby lives with its mother until it is a year old.
Relatives: Pandas look like bears but are related to raccoons.
Super-Duper Fact: A panda has a bone growing out of each wrist that helps it pick up food easily.

Platypus Facts

Habitat: The platypus lives in Australia.
Size: Platypuses grow from 16 to 22 in. (41 to 56 cm.) long, including a tail of 4 or 5 in. (10 to 13 cm.).
Food: The platypus uses its bill to search the bottoms of rivers for shrimp, worms, and crayfish.
Babies: The platypus is a monotreme. This means it is one of the few mammals that lay eggs.
Enemies: The male platypus has a curved fang, called a poison spur, attached to its back legs. He uses this spur as defense.
Super-Duper Fact: The platypus is an unusual mammal because it has webbed feet!

Rhinoceros Facts

Habitat: There are five species of rhinoceros: Sumatran, Indian, Javan, black, and white. Indian rhinos are found in Nepal. Black and white rhinos live in Africa.

Food: Rhinos are herbivores. This means that they eat plants.

Size: Rhinos can weigh 3,500 lbs. (1,589 kg.) and stand five ft. (2.2 m.) tall.

Endangered: All types of rhinos are in danger of extinction.

Senses: Rhinos have poor sight but a good sense of smell.

Speed: Rhinos can reach a speed of 35 mph (55 kph).

Super-Duper Fact: The rhino's horn is made of glued-together hair.

Sloth Facts

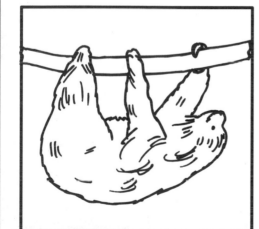

Habitat: Two-toed sloths live in dense forests of South America.

Food: Sloths eat leaves and flowers of the cecropia tree.

Babies: Baby sloths are born with ready claws.

Camouflage: Algae grows along the sloth's hair strands, helping it blend in with the trees. During rainy weather, the sloth looks green. In drought, it's yellow.

Speed: Sloths move so slowly that it isn't easy to see them moving in the trees.

Super-Duper Fact: Three kinds of moths, certain beetles, and many mites live in the sloth's colorful fur!

Animal A to Z List

A: Aardvark, Alpaca, Antelope, Ape
B: Bat, Bear, Bison, Buffalo
C: Camel, Cheetah, Chimpanzee, Cougar, Coyote
D: Deer, Dolphin, Donkey
E: Elephant, Elk, Ermine
F: Ferret, Flying Fox, Fox
G: Gazelle, Gerbil, Gibbon, Giraffe, Goat, Gorilla
H: Hamster, Hare, Hippopotamus, Horse, Hyena, Hyrax
I: Ibex, Insect-eater
J: Jackal, Jaguar
K: Kangaroo, Koala
L: Lemur, Leopard, Lion, Llama, Lynx
M: Mice, Mink, Mole, Mongoose, Monkey, Moose
N: Nyala (type of antelope)
O: Okapi, Opossum, Orangutan, Otter
P: Panda, Pig, Platypus, Polecat, Porcupine, Porpoise
R: Rabbit, Raccoon, Rat, Reindeer, Rhinoceros, Rodent
S: Sea Lion, Seal, Sheep, Shrew, Skunk, Sloth, Squirrel
T: Tapir, Tasmanian Wolf, Tiger
U: Ungulate, Unicorn
V: Vicuña
W: Wallaby, Walrus, Weasel, Whale, Wolverine, Wolf
Y: Yak
Z: Zebra, Zebu

Amazing Animals! © 1998 Monday Morning Books, Inc.

Nonfiction Resources

• *Album of North American Animals* by Vera Dugdale, illustrated by Clark Bronson (Rand McNally, 1966).

• *Amazing Animal Disguises* by Sandie Sowler (Knopf, 1992).

• *Amazing Bats* by Frank Greenaway (Knopf, 1991).

• *Amazing Mammals* by Alexandra Parsons, photographs by Jerry Young (Knopf, 1990).

• *Animal Camouflage: A Closer Look* by Joyce Powzyk (Bradbury, 1990).

• *Armadillos, Anteaters, and Sloths* by Jane E. Hartman (Holiday House, 1980).

• *The Australian Echidna* by Eleanor Stodart (Houghton Mifflin, 1991).

• *The Baby Zoo* by Bruce McMillan (Scholastic, 1992).

• *Bats in the Night* by George Laycock (Four Winds Press, 1981).

• *Big Cats* by Seymour Simon (HarperCollins, 1992).

• *Camels* by John Bonnett Wexo (Creative Education, 1989).

• *Dog* by Juliet Clutton-Brock (Knopf, 1991).

• *Great Mammals* by Lindsay Knight (Weldon Owen, 1992).

• *Hide and Seek*, edited by Jennifer Coldrey and Karen Goldie-Morrison (G. P. Putnam's Sons, 1986).

• *How Animals Hide* by Robert McClung (National Geographic Society, 1973).

• *How to Hide a Polar Bear and Other Mammals* by Ruth Heller (Grosset & Dunlap, 1985).

• *Joey: The Story of a Baby Kangaroo* by Hope Ryden (Tambourine, 1994).

• *Llama* by Caroline Arnold, photographs by Richard Hewett (Morrow, 1988). This team also wrote *Camel, Giraffe, Kangaroo, Koala, Penguin,* and *Zebra.*

• *Meet the Opossum* by Leonard Lee Rue III (Dodd, Mead, 1983).

• *Mind-Blowing Mammals* by Leslie Elliott (Sterling, 1994).

• *Saving Endangered Mammals* by Thane Maynard (Franklin Watts, 1992).

• *Those Amazing Bats* by Cheryl Mays Halton (Dillon, 1991).

• *Tiger, Tiger Growing Up....* by Joan Hewett, photographs by Richard Hewett (Clarion, 1993).

• *Warm-Blooded Animals* by Maurice Burton (Oribs, 1985).

• *Why Mammals Have Fur* by Dorothy Hinshaw Patent, photographs by William Muñoz (Dutton, 1995).

• *The Wildlife Atlas* by Sylvia A. Johnson, illustrated by Alcuin C. Dornisch (Lerner, 1977).

• *Zebras* by Linda C. Wood (Wildlife Education, 1993).

Amazing Animals! © 1998 Monday Morning Books, Inc.

Web Site Addresses

Camel Web Sites
• Bactrian Camel
hittp://www.med.usf.edu/NINA/park/asian/camel.html
• Mongolia
http://www.halcyon.com/mongolia/camels.html

Chimpanzee Web Sites
• Sea World: BuschGardens
Animal Bytes: Chimpanzee
http://www.bev.net/education/SeaWorld/
animal_bytes/chimpanzeeab.html

Echidna Web Sites
• Echidna (A-kid-na)
http://www.ozramp.net.au/~senani/
echidna.htm
• Short-nosed Anteater or Echidna
http://www.birminghamzoo.com/ao/
mammal/echidna.htm

Elephant Web Sites
• South African Bush Elephant
http://www.memo.com/zoo/exhibits/
elephant.html
• The African Elephant
http://frank.mtsu.edu/~jpurcell/Walker/Wildlife/
elefant.html

Platypus Web Sites
• The Platypus
http://www.ozemail.com/au/~knewhous/
platypus.htm

Tiger Web Sites
• The Tiger Information Center
http://www.5tigers.org

• The best efforts have been made to find current Web
sites, however Web sites sometimes change. In addition
to using these sites, also try keyword searches, such as
zoos or specific animal names.